52 Affirmations for School Librarians: Trace your way to purposeful days

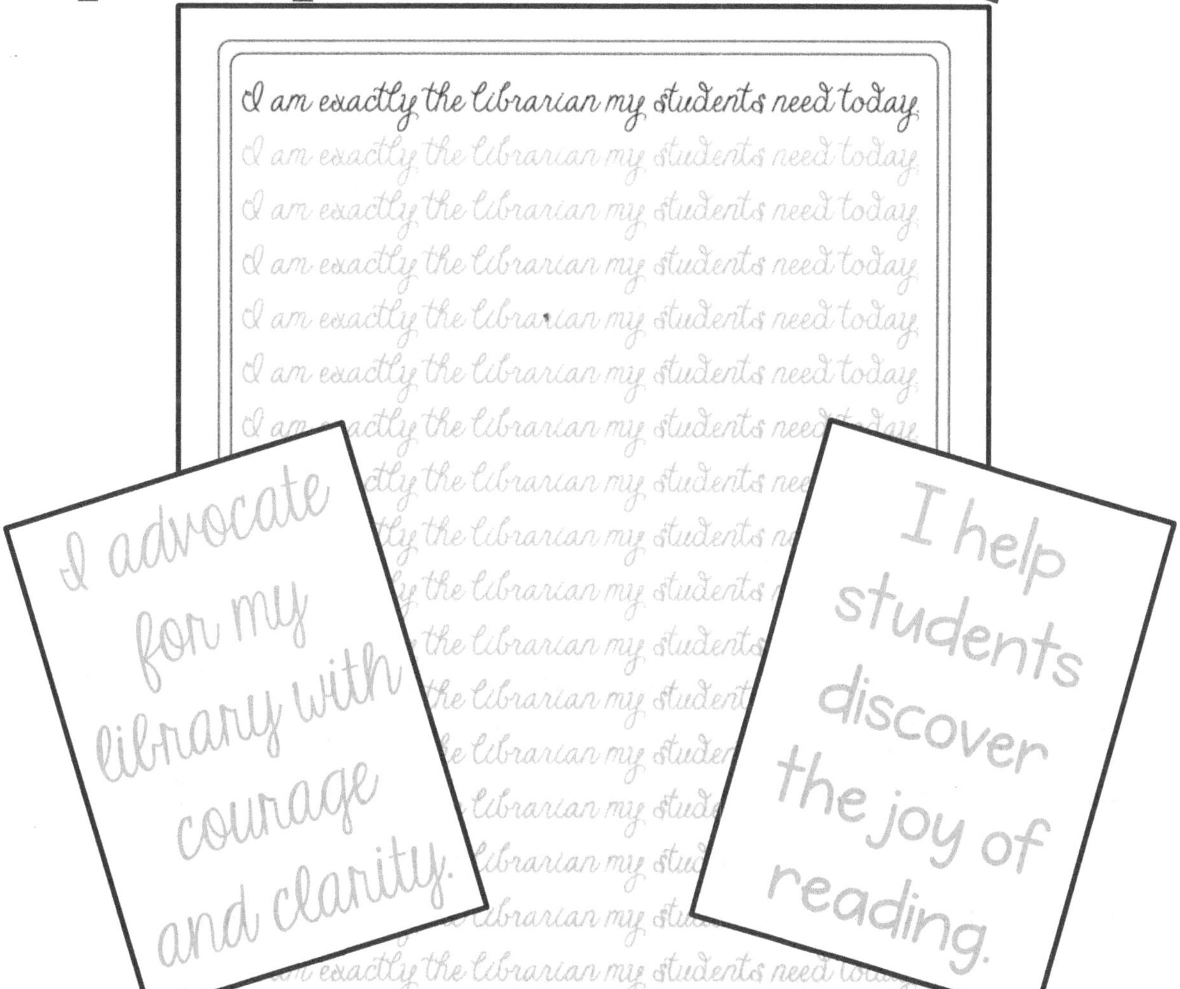

by Cari White
©Cari White, 2025-present

© Cari White 2025-present. All rights reserved.

All rights reserved. No part of this publication may be reproduced, distributed, or transmitted in any form or by any means. This includes photocopying, recording, or other electronic or mechanical methods without prior permission of the publisher, except in the case of brief quotations embodied in critical reviews and other noncommercial uses permitted by copyright law. All fonts are used by commercial license from Kimberly Geswein Fonts.

No part of this product may be used or reproduced for commercial use.

Contact the author :
LibraryLearners.com

How this book will help you

Affirmations

Affirmations can be a powerful, steadying tool for school librarians, especially in a role that asks you to juggle instruction, technology, collection management, and the emotional needs of hundreds of students. Taking a moment to speak a positive, intentional phrase helps you reset your mindset, reduce stress, and remember your purpose, even on the busiest days.

Affirmations can boost your confidence when you're leading lessons, advocating for your library program, or navigating tight schedules and shifting expectations. They remind you that the work you do matters, that you are capable, and that you deserve the same encouragement you give to your students. Over time, repeated affirmations will strengthen your resilience, helping you show up with clarity, calm, and compassion for yourself and your school community.

Handwriting

Repeatedly hand-writing affirmations adds an extra layer of power and intention to the practice. The physical act of writing slows your mind down just enough to focus on each word, helping the message sink in more deeply than when you simply think or speak it. As your hand forms each letter, you're creating a muscle-memory connection that reinforces the belief you're working to build.

Over time, these written affirmations create a visual record of your growth with pages that show your commitment, your hopes, and your resilience. The routine itself becomes grounding, a quiet moment of reflection that trains your brain to shift away from self-doubt and toward a stronger, kinder inner voice.

How to use this book

Full page repetition

The next 52 pages provide 52 different affirmations in 10 different fonts for you to trace over with your favorite pens. You may choose to focus on one affirmation per week for a year. Use as much or as little color as you'd like. If you are using pens that tend to bleed through the page, you might want to keep a sheet of printer paper in your book, to slide under the page that you're writing on.

Cut-apart notes

Pages 109 - 133 provide you with affirmation notes that you can trace over, cut apart and either use as a bookmark or post in a place where you will see it and repeat it, like:

* on your bathroom mirror
* at your desk
* on your computer monitor or laptop keyboard
* inside your planner
* on the dashboard of your car
* in a book you open often
* in your ID badge holder
* on the wall near your circulation desk
* on the door to your library office
* inside a drawer that you open every morning
* inside a cabinet door in your library workroom

May these pages remind you that you are changing the world every day in your school library. You are worthy of more appreciation and recognition than you will ever receive on your campus.

I create a welcoming space where every student feels seen.

I create a welcoming space where every student feels seen.

I create a welcoming space where every student feels seen.

I create a welcoming space where every student feels seen.

I create a welcoming space where every student feels seen.

I create a welcoming space where every student feels seen.

I create a welcoming space where every student feels seen.

I create a welcoming space where every student feels seen.

I create a welcoming space where every student feels seen.

I create a welcoming space where every student feels seen.

I create a welcoming space where every student feels seen.

I create a welcoming space where every student feels seen.

I create a welcoming space where every student feels seen.

I create a welcoming space where every student feels seen.

I create a welcoming space where every student feels seen.

I create a welcoming space where every student feels seen.

I create a welcoming space where every student feels seen.

I help students discover books that change their lives.

I help students discover books that change their lives.
I help students discover books that change their lives.
I help students discover books that change their lives.
I help students discover books that change their lives.
I help students discover books that change their lives.
I help students discover books that change their lives.
I help students discover books that change their lives.
I help students discover books that change their lives.
I help students discover books that change their lives.
I help students discover books that change their lives.
I help students discover books that change their lives.
I help students discover books that change their lives.
I help students discover books that change their lives.
I help students discover books that change their lives.
I help students discover books that change their lives.
I help students discover books that change their lives.

I am the heart of my school's reading community.

I am the heart of my school's reading community.
I am the heart of my school's reading community.
I am the heart of my school's reading community.
I am the heart of my school's reading community.
I am the heart of my school's reading community.
I am the heart of my school's reading community.
I am the heart of my school's reading community.
I am the heart of my school's reading community.
I am the heart of my school's reading community.
I am the heart of my school's reading community.
I am the heart of my school's reading community.
I am the heart of my school's reading community.
I am the heart of my school's reading community.
I am the heart of my school's reading community.
I am the heart of my school's reading community.

I guide students toward curiosity and lifelong learning.

I guide students toward curiosity and lifelong learning.

I guide students toward curiosity and lifelong learning.

I guide students toward curiosity and lifelong learning.

I guide students toward curiosity and lifelong learning.

I guide students toward curiosity and lifelong learning.

I guide students toward curiosity and lifelong learning.

I guide students toward curiosity and lifelong learning.

I guide students toward curiosity and lifelong learning.

I guide students toward curiosity and lifelong learning.

I guide students toward curiosity and lifelong learning.

I guide students toward curiosity and lifelong learning.

I guide students toward curiosity and lifelong learning.

I guide students toward curiosity and lifelong learning.

I guide students toward curiosity and lifelong learning.

I guide students toward curiosity and lifelong learning.

I am patient with myself as I juggle many roles.

I am patient with myself as I juggle many roles.

I am patient with myself as I juggle many roles.

I am patient with myself as I juggle many roles.

I am patient with myself as I juggle many roles.

I am patient with myself as I juggle many roles.

I am patient with myself as I juggle many roles.

I am patient with myself as I juggle many roles.

I am patient with myself as I juggle many roles.

I am patient with myself as I juggle many roles.

I am patient with myself as I juggle many roles.

I am patient with myself as I juggle many roles.

I am patient with myself as I juggle many roles.

I am patient with myself as I juggle many roles.

I am patient with myself as I juggle many roles.

I am patient with myself as I juggle many roles.

I support teachers, students, and staff with care and expertise.

I support teachers, students, and staff with care and expertise.

I support teachers, students, and staff with care and expertise.

I support teachers, students, and staff with care and expertise.

I support teachers, students, and staff with care and expertise.

I support teachers, students, and staff with care and expertise.

I support teachers, students, and staff with care and expertise.

I support teachers, students, and staff with care and expertise.

I support teachers, students, and staff with care and expertise.

I support teachers, students, and staff with care and expertise.

I support teachers, students, and staff with care and expertise.

I support teachers, students, and staff with care and expertise.

I support teachers, students, and staff with care and expertise.

I support teachers, students, and staff with care and expertise.

I support teachers, students, and staff with care and expertise.

I support teachers, students, and staff with care and expertise.

I am organized, resourceful, and capable.

I am organized, resourceful, and capable.
I am organized, resourceful, and capable.
I am organized, resourceful, and capable.
I am organized, resourceful, and capable.
I am organized, resourceful, and capable.
I am organized, resourceful, and capable.
I am organized, resourceful, and capable.
I am organized, resourceful, and capable.
I am organized, resourceful, and capable.
I am organized, resourceful, and capable.
I am organized, resourceful, and capable.
I am organized, resourceful, and capable.
I am organized, resourceful, and capable.
I am organized, resourceful, and capable.
I am organized, resourceful, and capable.

I bring calm and structure to busy library days.

I bring calm and structure to busy library days.

I bring calm and structure to busy library days.

I bring calm and structure to busy library days.

I bring calm and structure to busy library days.

I bring calm and structure to busy library days.

I bring calm and structure to busy library days.

I bring calm and structure to busy library days.

I bring calm and structure to busy library days.

I bring calm and structure to busy library days.

I bring calm and structure to busy library days.

I bring calm and structure to busy library days.

I bring calm and structure to busy library days.

I bring calm and structure to busy library days.

I bring calm and structure to busy library days.

I bring calm and structure to busy library days.

I bring calm and structure to busy library days.

I inspire my students simply by sharing my love of reading.

I curate materials that open doors for every learner.

I curate materials that open doors for every learner.

I curate materials that open doors for every learner.

I curate materials that open doors for every learner.

I curate materials that open doors for every learner.

I curate materials that open doors for every learner.

I curate materials that open doors for every learner.

I curate materials that open doors for every learner.

I curate materials that open doors for every learner.

I curate materials that open doors for every learner.

I curate materials that open doors for every learner.

I curate materials that open doors for every learner.

I curate materials that open doors for every learner.

I curate materials that open doors for every learner.

I curate materials that open doors for every learner.

I curate materials that open doors for every learner.

I curate materials that open doors for every learner.

I use my creativity to make the library magical.

I use my creativity to make the library magical.
I use my creativity to make the library magical.
I use my creativity to make the library magical.
I use my creativity to make the library magical.
I use my creativity to make the library magical.
I use my creativity to make the library magical.
I use my creativity to make the library magical.
I use my creativity to make the library magical.
I use my creativity to make the library magical.
I use my creativity to make the library magical.
I use my creativity to make the library magical.
I use my creativity to make the library magical.
I use my creativity to make the library magical.
I use my creativity to make the library magical.
I use my creativity to make the library magical.
I use my creativity to make the library magical.

I am proud of the difference I make in students' lives.

I am proud of the difference I make in students' lives.

I am proud of the difference I make in students' lives.

I am proud of the difference I make in students' lives.

I am proud of the difference I make in students' lives.

I am proud of the difference I make in students' lives.

I am proud of the difference I make in students' lives.

I am proud of the difference I make in students' lives.

I am proud of the difference I make in students' lives.

I am proud of the difference I make in students' lives.

I am proud of the difference I make in students' lives.

I am proud of the difference I make in students' lives.

I am proud of the difference I make in students' lives.

I am proud of the difference I make in students' lives.

I am proud of the difference I make in students' lives.

I am proud of the difference I make in students' lives.

I am continually learning and growing as a librarian.

I am continually learning and growing as a librarian.

I am continually learning and growing as a librarian.

I am continually learning and growing as a librarian.

I am continually learning and growing as a librarian.

I am continually learning and growing as a librarian.

I am continually learning and growing as a librarian.

I am continually learning and growing as a librarian.

I am continually learning and growing as a librarian.

I am continually learning and growing as a librarian.

I am continually learning and growing as a librarian.

I am continually learning and growing as a librarian.

I am continually learning and growing as a librarian.

I am continually learning and growing as a librarian.

I am continually learning and growing as a librarian.

I am continually learning and growing as a librarian.

I am continually learning and growing as a librarian.

I am flexible and can adapt to any challenge.

I am flexible and can adapt to any challenge.
I am flexible and can adapt to any challenge.
I am flexible and can adapt to any challenge.
I am flexible and can adapt to any challenge.
I am flexible and can adapt to any challenge.
I am flexible and can adapt to any challenge.
I am flexible and can adapt to any challenge.
I am flexible and can adapt to any challenge.
I am flexible and can adapt to any challenge.
I am flexible and can adapt to any challenge.
I am flexible and can adapt to any challenge.
I am flexible and can adapt to any challenge.
I am flexible and can adapt to any challenge.
I am flexible and can adapt to any challenge.
I am flexible and can adapt to any challenge.

honor the unique needs of each student who walks through my doors.

honor the unique needs of each student who walks through my doors.

honor the unique needs of each student who walks through my doors.

honor the unique needs of each student who walks through my doors.

honor the unique needs of each student who walks through my doors.

honor the unique needs of each student who walks through my doors.

honor the unique needs of each student who walks through my doors.

honor the unique needs of each student who walks through my doors.

honor the unique needs of each student who walks through my doors.

honor the unique needs of each student who walks through my doors.

honor the unique needs of each student who walks through my doors.

honor the unique needs of each student who walks through my doors.

honor the unique needs of each student who walks through my doors.

honor the unique needs of each student who walks through my doors.

honor the unique needs of each student who walks through my doors.

I build connections that support strong reading habits.

I build connections that support strong reading habits.
I build connections that support strong reading habits.
I build connections that support strong reading habits.
I build connections that support strong reading habits.
I build connections that support strong reading habits.
I build connections that support strong reading habits.
I build connections that support strong reading habits.
I build connections that support strong reading habits.
I build connections that support strong reading habits.
I build connections that support strong reading habits.
I build connections that support strong reading habits.
I build connections that support strong reading habits.
I build connections that support strong reading habits.
I build connections that support strong reading habits.
I build connections that support strong reading habits.

I create lessons that spark joy and engagement.
I create lessons that spark joy and engagement.
I create lessons that spark joy and engagement.
I create lessons that spark joy and engagement.
I create lessons that spark joy and engagement.
I create lessons that spark joy and engagement.
I create lessons that spark joy and engagement.
I create lessons that spark joy and engagement.
I create lessons that spark joy and engagement.
I create lessons that spark joy and engagement.
I create lessons that spark joy and engagement.
I create lessons that spark joy and engagement.
I create lessons that spark joy and engagement.
I create lessons that spark joy and engagement.
I create lessons that spark joy and engagement.
I create lessons that spark joy and engagement.
I create lessons that spark joy and engagement.

I am a confident, capable educator.

I am a confident, capable educator.
I am a confident, capable educator.
I am a confident, capable educator.
I am a confident, capable educator.
I am a confident, capable educator.
I am a confident, capable educator.
I am a confident, capable educator.
I am a confident, capable educator.
I am a confident, capable educator.
I am a confident, capable educator.
I am a confident, capable educator.
I am a confident, capable educator.
I am a confident, capable educator.
I am a confident, capable educator.
I am a confident, capable educator.
I am a confident, capable educator.

I help students feel safe, welcome, and encouraged.

I help students feel safe, welcome, and encouraged.

I help students feel safe, welcome, and encouraged.

I help students feel safe, welcome, and encouraged.

I help students feel safe, welcome, and encouraged.

I help students feel safe, welcome, and encouraged.

I help students feel safe, welcome, and encouraged.

I help students feel safe, welcome, and encouraged.

I help students feel safe, welcome, and encouraged.

I help students feel safe, welcome, and encouraged.

I help students feel safe, welcome, and encouraged.

I help students feel safe, welcome, and encouraged.

I help students feel safe, welcome, and encouraged.

I help students feel safe, welcome, and encouraged.

I help students feel safe, welcome, and encouraged.

I help students feel safe, welcome, and encouraged.

I bring kindness and compassion into every interaction.

I bring kindness and compassion into every interaction.

I bring kindness and compassion into every interaction.

I bring kindness and compassion into every interaction.

I bring kindness and compassion into every interaction.

I bring kindness and compassion into every interaction.

I bring kindness and compassion into every interaction.

I bring kindness and compassion into every interaction.

I bring kindness and compassion into every interaction.

I bring kindness and compassion into every interaction.

I bring kindness and compassion into every interaction.

I bring kindness and compassion into every interaction.

I bring kindness and compassion into every interaction.

I bring kindness and compassion into every interaction.

I bring kindness and compassion into every interaction.

I bring kindness and compassion into every interaction.

I bring kindness and compassion into every interaction.

I balance structure with creativity in my library.

I balance structure with creativity in my library.

I balance structure with creativity in my library.

I balance structure with creativity in my library.

I balance structure with creativity in my library.

I balance structure with creativity in my library.

I balance structure with creativity in my library.

I balance structure with creativity in my library.

I balance structure with creativity in my library.

I balance structure with creativity in my library.

I balance structure with creativity in my library.

I balance structure with creativity in my library.

I balance structure with creativity in my library.

I balance structure with creativity in my library.

I balance structure with creativity in my library.

I balance structure with creativity in my library.

I help students discover the joy of reading.

I help students discover the joy of reading.
I help students discover the joy of reading.
I help students discover the joy of reading.
I help students discover the joy of reading.
I help students discover the joy of reading.
I help students discover the joy of reading.
I help students discover the joy of reading.
I help students discover the joy of reading.
I help students discover the joy of reading.
I help students discover the joy of reading.
I help students discover the joy of reading.
I help students discover the joy of reading.
I help students discover the joy of reading.
I help students discover the joy of reading.
I help students discover the joy of reading.
I help students discover the joy of reading.

I am valued, even when my work goes unseen.

I am valued, even when my work goes unseen.

I am valued, even when my work goes unseen.

I am valued, even when my work goes unseen.

I am valued, even when my work goes unseen.

I am valued, even when my work goes unseen.

I am valued, even when my work goes unseen.

I am valued, even when my work goes unseen.

I am valued, even when my work goes unseen.

I am valued, even when my work goes unseen.

I am valued, even when my work goes unseen.

I am valued, even when my work goes unseen.

I am valued, even when my work goes unseen.

I am valued, even when my work goes unseen.

I am valued, even when my work goes unseen.

I am valued, even when my work goes unseen.

I am valued, even when my work goes unseen.

I am valued, even when my work goes unseen.

I create moments of joy for students every day.

I create moments of joy for students every day.

I create moments of joy for students every day.

I create moments of joy for students every day.

I create moments of joy for students every day.

I create moments of joy for students every day.

I create moments of joy for students every day.

I create moments of joy for students every day.

I create moments of joy for students every day.

I create moments of joy for students every day.

I create moments of joy for students every day.

I create moments of joy for students every day.

I create moments of joy for students every day.

I create moments of joy for students every day.

I create moments of joy for students every day.

I create moments of joy for students every day.

I create moments of joy for students every day.

I teach skills that empower students for life.

I teach skills that empower students for life.

I teach skills that empower students for life.

I teach skills that empower students for life.

I teach skills that empower students for life.

I teach skills that empower students for life.

I teach skills that empower students for life.

I teach skills that empower students for life.

I teach skills that empower students for life.

I teach skills that empower students for life.

I teach skills that empower students for life.

I teach skills that empower students for life.

I teach skills that empower students for life.

I teach skills that empower students for life.

I teach skills that empower students for life.

I teach skills that empower students for life.

I teach skills that empower students for life.

I advocate for my library with courage and clarity.

I advocate for my library with courage and clarity.
I advocate for my library with courage and clarity.
I advocate for my library with courage and clarity.
I advocate for my library with courage and clarity.
I advocate for my library with courage and clarity.
I advocate for my library with courage and clarity.
I advocate for my library with courage and clarity.
I advocate for my library with courage and clarity.
I advocate for my library with courage and clarity.
I advocate for my library with courage and clarity.
I advocate for my library with courage and clarity.
I advocate for my library with courage and clarity.
I advocate for my library with courage and clarity.
I advocate for my library with courage and clarity.
I advocate for my library with courage and clarity.
I advocate for my library with courage and clarity.
I advocate for my library with courage and clarity.

I am a calm, encouraging presence for my school community.

I am a calm, encouraging presence for my school community.
I am a calm, encouraging presence for my school community.
I am a calm, encouraging presence for my school community.
I am a calm, encouraging presence for my school community.
I am a calm, encouraging presence for my school community.
I am a calm, encouraging presence for my school community.
I am a calm, encouraging presence for my school community.
I am a calm, encouraging presence for my school community.
I am a calm, encouraging presence for my school community.
I am a calm, encouraging presence for my school community.
I am a calm, encouraging presence for my school community.
I am a calm, encouraging presence for my school community.
I am a calm, encouraging presence for my school community.
I am a calm, encouraging presence for my school community.
I am a calm, encouraging presence for my school community.
I am a calm, encouraging presence for my school community.

I bring order to chaos with grace and humor.

I bring order to chaos with grace and humor.
I bring order to chaos with grace and humor.
I bring order to chaos with grace and humor.
I bring order to chaos with grace and humor.
I bring order to chaos with grace and humor.
I bring order to chaos with grace and humor.
I bring order to chaos with grace and humor.
I bring order to chaos with grace and humor.
I bring order to chaos with grace and humor.
I bring order to chaos with grace and humor.
I bring order to chaos with grace and humor.
I bring order to chaos with grace and humor.
I bring order to chaos with grace and humor.
I bring order to chaos with grace and humor.
I bring order to chaos with grace and humor.
I bring order to chaos with grace and humor.

I celebrate every small step toward reading growth.

I celebrate every small step toward reading growth.

I celebrate every small step toward reading growth.

I celebrate every small step toward reading growth.

I celebrate every small step toward reading growth.

I celebrate every small step toward reading growth.

I celebrate every small step toward reading growth.

I celebrate every small step toward reading growth.

I celebrate every small step toward reading growth.

I celebrate every small step toward reading growth.

I celebrate every small step toward reading growth.

I celebrate every small step toward reading growth.

I celebrate every small step toward reading growth.

I celebrate every small step toward reading growth.

I celebrate every small step toward reading growth.

I celebrate every small step toward reading growth.

I am patient with students who need extra support.

I am patient with students who need extra support.

I am patient with students who need extra support.

I am patient with students who need extra support.

I am patient with students who need extra support.

I am patient with students who need extra support.

I am patient with students who need extra support.

I am patient with students who need extra support.

I am patient with students who need extra support.

I am patient with students who need extra support.

I am patient with students who need extra support.

I am patient with students who need extra support.

I am patient with students who need extra support.

I am patient with students who need extra support.

I am patient with students who need extra support.

I am patient with students who need extra support.

I am patient with students who need extra support.

I choose compassion over frustration.

I choose compassion over frustration.
I choose compassion over frustration.
I choose compassion over frustration.
I choose compassion over frustration.
I choose compassion over frustration.
I choose compassion over frustration.
I choose compassion over frustration.
I choose compassion over frustration.
I choose compassion over frustration.
I choose compassion over frustration.
I choose compassion over frustration.
I choose compassion over frustration.
I choose compassion over frustration.
I choose compassion over frustration.
I choose compassion over frustration.
I choose compassion over frustration.

I help students discover new ideas and interests.

I help students discover new ideas and interests.

I help students discover new ideas and interests.

I help students discover new ideas and interests.

I help students discover new ideas and interests.

I help students discover new ideas and interests.

I help students discover new ideas and interests.

I help students discover new ideas and interests.

I help students discover new ideas and interests.

I help students discover new ideas and interests.

I help students discover new ideas and interests.

I help students discover new ideas and interests.

I help students discover new ideas and interests.

I help students discover new ideas and interests.

I help students discover new ideas and interests.

I help students discover new ideas and interests.

I help students discover new ideas and interests.

foster curiosity through books and research skills.

foster curiosity through books and research skills.
foster curiosity through books and research skills.
foster curiosity through books and research skills.
foster curiosity through books and research skills.
foster curiosity through books and research skills.
foster curiosity through books and research skills.
foster curiosity through books and research skills.
foster curiosity through books and research skills.
foster curiosity through books and research skills.
foster curiosity through books and research skills.
foster curiosity through books and research skills.
foster curiosity through books and research skills.
foster curiosity through books and research skills.
foster curiosity through books and research skills.
foster curiosity through books and research skills.
foster curiosity through books and research skills.

I am proud of the safe & supportive library environment I create.

I am proud of the safe & supportive library environment I create.

I am proud of the safe & supportive library environment I create.

I am proud of the safe & supportive library environment I create.

I am proud of the safe & supportive library environment I create.

I am proud of the safe & supportive library environment I create.

I am proud of the safe & supportive library environment I create.

I am proud of the safe & supportive library environment I create.

I am proud of the safe & supportive library environment I create.

I am proud of the safe & supportive library environment I create.

I am proud of the safe & supportive library environment I create.

I am proud of the safe & supportive library environment I create.

I am proud of the safe & supportive library environment I create.

I am proud of the safe & supportive library environment I create.

I am proud of the safe & supportive library environment I create.

I am proud of the safe & supportive library environment I create.

I am proud of the safe & supportive library environment I create.

I approach challenges with confidence and creativity.

I approach challenges with confidence and creativity.

I approach challenges with confidence and creativity.

I approach challenges with confidence and creativity.

I approach challenges with confidence and creativity.

I approach challenges with confidence and creativity.

I approach challenges with confidence and creativity.

I approach challenges with confidence and creativity.

I approach challenges with confidence and creativity.

I approach challenges with confidence and creativity.

I approach challenges with confidence and creativity.

I approach challenges with confidence and creativity.

I approach challenges with confidence and creativity.

I approach challenges with confidence and creativity.

I approach challenges with confidence and creativity.

I approach challenges with confidence and creativity.

I approach challenges with confidence and creativity.

I don't need to do everything, just the next right thing.

I don't need to do everything, just the next right thing.
I don't need to do everything, just the next right thing.
I don't need to do everything, just the next right thing.
I don't need to do everything, just the next right thing.
I don't need to do everything, just the next right thing.
I don't need to do everything, just the next right thing.
I don't need to do everything, just the next right thing.
I don't need to do everything, just the next right thing.
I don't need to do everything, just the next right thing.
I don't need to do everything, just the next right thing.
I don't need to do everything, just the next right thing.
I don't need to do everything, just the next right thing.
I don't need to do everything, just the next right thing.
I don't need to do everything, just the next right thing.
I don't need to do everything, just the next right thing.
I don't need to do everything, just the next right thing.

I am a reading role model for my students.

I am a reading role model for my students.
I am a reading role model for my students.
I am a reading role model for my students.
I am a reading role model for my students.
I am a reading role model for my students.
I am a reading role model for my students.
I am a reading role model for my students.
I am a reading role model for my students.
I am a reading role model for my students.
I am a reading role model for my students.
I am a reading role model for my students.
I am a reading role model for my students.
I am a reading role model for my students.
I am a reading role model for my students.
I am a reading role model for my students.
I am a reading role model for my students.

I nurture a love of learning in my students.

I nurture a love of learning in my students.
I nurture a love of learning in my students.
I nurture a love of learning in my students.
I nurture a love of learning in my students.
I nurture a love of learning in my students.
I nurture a love of learning in my students.
I nurture a love of learning in my students.
I nurture a love of learning in my students.
I nurture a love of learning in my students.
I nurture a love of learning in my students.
I nurture a love of learning in my students.
I nurture a love of learning in my students.
I nurture a love of learning in my students.
I nurture a love of learning in my students.
I nurture a love of learning in my students.
I nurture a love of learning in my students.

I bring warmth and joy to my school.

I know that every book I share has potential to inspire.

I know that every book I share has potential to inspire.

I know that every book I share has potential to inspire.

I know that every book I share has potential to inspire.

I know that every book I share has potential to inspire.

I know that every book I share has potential to inspire.

I know that every book I share has potential to inspire.

I know that every book I share has potential to inspire.

I know that every book I share has potential to inspire.

I know that every book I share has potential to inspire.

I know that every book I share has potential to inspire.

I know that every book I share has potential to inspire.

I know that every book I share has potential to inspire.

I know that every book I share has potential to inspire.

I know that every book I share has potential to inspire.

I know that every book I share has potential to inspire.

I embrace change as part of my growth.

I embrace change as part of my growth.

I embrace change as part of my growth.

I embrace change as part of my growth.

I embrace change as part of my growth.

I embrace change as part of my growth.

I embrace change as part of my growth.

I embrace change as part of my growth.

I embrace change as part of my growth.

I embrace change as part of my growth.

I embrace change as part of my growth.

I embrace change as part of my growth.

I embrace change as part of my growth.

I embrace change as part of my growth.

I embrace change as part of my growth.

I embrace change as part of my growth.

I enrich my school through thoughtful library instruction.

I enrich my school through thoughtful library instruction.

I enrich my school through thoughtful library instruction.

I enrich my school through thoughtful library instruction.

I enrich my school through thoughtful library instruction.

I enrich my school through thoughtful library instruction.

I enrich my school through thoughtful library instruction.

I enrich my school through thoughtful library instruction.

I enrich my school through thoughtful library instruction.

I enrich my school through thoughtful library instruction.

I enrich my school through thoughtful library instruction.

I enrich my school through thoughtful library instruction.

I enrich my school through thoughtful library instruction.

I enrich my school through thoughtful library instruction.

I enrich my school through thoughtful library instruction.

I enrich my school through thoughtful library instruction.

I help students feel capable, confident, and curious.

I help students feel capable, confident, and curious.

I help students feel capable, confident, and curious.

I help students feel capable, confident, and curious.

I help students feel capable, confident, and curious.

I help students feel capable, confident, and curious.

I help students feel capable, confident, and curious.

I help students feel capable, confident, and curious.

I help students feel capable, confident, and curious.

I help students feel capable, confident, and curious.

I help students feel capable, confident, and curious.

I help students feel capable, confident, and curious.

I help students feel capable, confident, and curious.

I help students feel capable, confident, and curious.

I help students feel capable, confident, and curious.

I help students feel capable, confident, and curious.

I help students feel capable, confident, and curious.

I honor my boundaries and protect my energy.

I honor my boundaries and protect my energy.
I honor my boundaries and protect my energy.
I honor my boundaries and protect my energy.
I honor my boundaries and protect my energy.
I honor my boundaries and protect my energy.
I honor my boundaries and protect my energy.
I honor my boundaries and protect my energy.
I honor my boundaries and protect my energy.
I honor my boundaries and protect my energy.
I honor my boundaries and protect my energy.
I honor my boundaries and protect my energy.
I honor my boundaries and protect my energy.
I honor my boundaries and protect my energy.
I honor my boundaries and protect my energy.
I honor my boundaries and protect my energy.

I bring people together through stories and shared experiences.

I bring people together through stories and shared experiences.

I bring people together through stories and shared experiences.

I bring people together through stories and shared experiences.

I bring people together through stories and shared experiences.

I bring people together through stories and shared experiences.

I bring people together through stories and shared experiences.

I bring people together through stories and shared experiences.

I bring people together through stories and shared experiences.

I bring people together through stories and shared experiences.

I bring people together through stories and shared experiences.

I bring people together through stories and shared experiences.

I bring people together through stories and shared experiences.

I bring people together through stories and shared experiences.

I bring people together through stories and shared experiences.

I bring people together through stories and shared experiences.

I bring people together through stories and shared experiences.

I nurture a culture of respect in my library.

I nurture a culture of respect in my library.
I nurture a culture of respect in my library.
I nurture a culture of respect in my library.
I nurture a culture of respect in my library.
I nurture a culture of respect in my library.
I nurture a culture of respect in my library.
I nurture a culture of respect in my library.
I nurture a culture of respect in my library.
I nurture a culture of respect in my library.
I nurture a culture of respect in my library.
I nurture a culture of respect in my library.
I nurture a culture of respect in my library.
I nurture a culture of respect in my library.
I nurture a culture of respect in my library.
I nurture a culture of respect in my library.

I give myself grace on difficult days.

I give myself grace on difficult days. (×18)

I am doing important and meaningful work.

I am doing important and meaningful work.
I am doing important and meaningful work.
I am doing important and meaningful work.
I am doing important and meaningful work.
I am doing important and meaningful work.
I am doing important and meaningful work.
I am doing important and meaningful work.
I am doing important and meaningful work.
I am doing important and meaningful work.
I am doing important and meaningful work.
I am doing important and meaningful work.
I am doing important and meaningful work.
I am doing important and meaningful work.
I am doing important and meaningful work.
I am doing important and meaningful work.
I am doing important and meaningful work.

I am exactly the librarian my students need today.

I am exactly the librarian my students need today.

I am exactly the librarian my students need today.

I am exactly the librarian my students need today.

I am exactly the librarian my students need today.

I am exactly the librarian my students need today.

I am exactly the librarian my students need today.

I am exactly the librarian my students need today.

I am exactly the librarian my students need today.

I am exactly the librarian my students need today.

I am exactly the librarian my students need today.

I am exactly the librarian my students need today.

I am exactly the librarian my students need today.

I am exactly the librarian my students need today.

I am exactly the librarian my students need today.

I am exactly the librarian my students need today.

I am exactly the librarian my students need today.

I am proud of the reader, leader, and librarian I am becoming.

I am proud of the reader, leader, and librarian I am becoming.

I am proud of the reader, leader, and librarian I am becoming.

I am proud of the reader, leader, and librarian I am becoming.

I am proud of the reader, leader, and librarian I am becoming.

I am proud of the reader, leader, and librarian I am becoming.

I am proud of the reader, leader, and librarian I am becoming.

I am proud of the reader, leader, and librarian I am becoming.

I am proud of the reader, leader, and librarian I am becoming.

I am proud of the reader, leader, and librarian I am becoming.

I am proud of the reader, leader, and librarian I am becoming.

I am proud of the reader, leader, and librarian I am becoming.

I am proud of the reader, leader, and librarian I am becoming.

I am proud of the reader, leader, and librarian I am becoming.

I am proud of the reader, leader, and librarian I am becoming.

I am proud of the reader, leader, and librarian I am becoming.

I am proud of the reader, leader, and librarian I am becoming.

I am grateful for the work I get to do each day.

I am grateful for the work I get to do each day.
I am grateful for the work I get to do each day.
I am grateful for the work I get to do each day.
I am grateful for the work I get to do each day.
I am grateful for the work I get to do each day.
I am grateful for the work I get to do each day.
I am grateful for the work I get to do each day.
I am grateful for the work I get to do each day.
I am grateful for the work I get to do each day.
I am grateful for the work I get to do each day.
I am grateful for the work I get to do each day.
I am grateful for the work I get to do each day.
I am grateful for the work I get to do each day.
I am grateful for the work I get to do each day.
I am grateful for the work I get to do each day.
I am grateful for the work I get to do each day.

I make thoughtful choices that benefit my learners.

I make thoughtful choices that benefit my learners.
I make thoughtful choices that benefit my learners.
I make thoughtful choices that benefit my learners.
I make thoughtful choices that benefit my learners.
I make thoughtful choices that benefit my learners.
I make thoughtful choices that benefit my learners.
I make thoughtful choices that benefit my learners.
I make thoughtful choices that benefit my learners.
I make thoughtful choices that benefit my learners.
I make thoughtful choices that benefit my learners.
I make thoughtful choices that benefit my learners.
I make thoughtful choices that benefit my learners.
I make thoughtful choices that benefit my learners.
I make thoughtful choices that benefit my learners.
I make thoughtful choices that benefit my learners.

I create a welcoming space where every student feels seen.

I help students discover books that change their lives.

I am the heart of my school's reading community.

I guide students toward curiosity and lifelong learning.

I am patient with myself as I juggle many roles.

I support teachers, students, and staff with care and expertise.

I am organized, resourceful, and capable.

I bring calm and structure to busy library days.

I inspire students simply by sharing my love of reading.

I curate materials that open doors for every learner.

I use my creativity to make the library magical.

I am proud of the difference I make in students' lives.

I am continually learning and growing as a librarian.	I am flexible and can adapt to any challenge.
I honor the unique needs of each student who walks through my doors.	I build connections that support strong reading habits.

I create lessons that spark joy and engagement.	I am a confident, capable educator.
I help students feel safe, welcomed, and encouraged.	I bring kindness and compassion into every interaction.

I balance structure with creativity in my library.	I help students discover the joy of reading.
I am valued, even when my work goes unseen.	I create moments of joy for students every day.

I teach skills that empower students for life.	I advocate for my library with courage and clarity.
I am a calm, encouraging presence for my school community.	I bring order to chaos with grace and humor.

I celebrate every small step toward reading growth.

I am patient with students who need extra support.

I choose compassion over frustration.

I help students discover new ideas and interests.

I foster curiosity through books and research skills.	I am proud of the safe & supportive library environment I create.
I approach challenges with confidence and creativity.	I don't need to do everything, just the next right thing.

I am a reading role model for my students.	I nurture a love of learning in my students.
I bring warmth and joy to my school.	I know that every book I share has potential to inspire.

I embrace change as part of my growth.	I enrich my school through thoughtful library instruction.
I help students feel capable, confident, and curious.	I honor my boundaries and protect my energy.

I bring people together through stories and shared experiences.	I nurture a culture of respect in my library.
I give myself grace on difficult days.	I am doing important and meaningful work.

I am exactly the librarian my students need today.

I am proud of the reader, leader, and librarian I am becoming.

I am grateful for the work I get to do each day.

I make thoughtful choices that benefit my learners.

Copyrighted Materials; All Rights Reserved
©Cari White, 2025-present

Thank you for your purchase and thank you for the work you do every day! You make the world a better place!

I'd love your feedback!

If you enjoyed this book, would you take a moment to leave a review on Amazon? Your review (whether it's a sentence or a paragraph) helps other librarians discover the book and supports the work that went into creating it.

Your voice truly makes a difference.
Thank you so much for reading and for sharing your thoughts!

LibraryLearners.com

Want a FREE librarian idea book you can use today?

Made in the USA
Coppell, TX
21 January 2026